BECAUSE I AM WOMAN: *Reflections of a Woman*

Because I Am Woman

JESSICA WOODRUFF

JESSICA WOODRUFF

Because I Am Woman copyright © 2019 by Jessica Woodruff. All rights reserved. Printed in the United States of America. No part of this book may be used or reproduced in any manner whatsoever without written permission except in the case of reprints in the context of reviews.

BIAW Books Publishing
Douglasville, GA

www.BIAW-Inc.org

Copyright © 2019 Jessica Woodruff
All rights reserved
ISBN-13: 978-1-7341284-0-6
ISBN-10: 1-7341284-0-2

Library of Congress Control Number: 2019915847

Because I Am Woman

Reflections of a Woman

by Jessica Woodruff

Published by BIAW Books
Atlanta

BECAUSE I AM WOMAN: *Reflections of a Woman*

To those who have been waiting to hear from me, here I speak.
To those that have been waiting to listen to me, here I tell.

-Jessica Nicole.

JESSICA WOODRUFF

BECAUSE I AM WOMAN: *Reflections of a Woman*

Table of Contents

Introduction to the..................................1

Woman I am...............................13

On my destined path............................21

Trying to discover......................................36

My true and genuine self.....................43

All the while I am......................................64

Battling within my own mind..............87

Fighting against the outside................109

World and perceived obstacles............122

But emerging ever-triumphant...........150

Because I Am Woman..........................165.

Introduction

First off, let me say this…it is not uncommon to run into personal obstacles when you set out on the true path of your purpose. So many setbacks (or what I like to call setups) and tests (precursors to testimonies) will be tossed at you. However, the most important thing you will ever do, aside from actually overcoming the obstacles in your way, is to make the decision to push through.

Honesty moment in 3…2…1…this book has definitely set me on a path to run into my own personal obstacles. The writing process in itself has been a long time coming; from changing the direction and concept that I originally chose, to doubting if it would even be worth the read for anyone. Self-doubt comes and tries to set-in in the most adverse ways, and it even set in when dealing with endeavors outside of the book that I tried to work on. Especially in my non-profit, Because I Am Woman, Inc. (BIAW-Inc.org), I have dealt with internal and external issues.

One of the issues I ran into was a perceived lack of support. I *want* to build a platform for women empowerment through workshops, classes, support groups, and on a grander scale, empowerment retreats and women's expos. But whenever the thought that I won't get the support I need creeps in, those concepts go from unfulfilled dreams to far-off fantasies.

Don't get me wrong, I have always had a support system, but it seemed to dwindle as I got older. Not because my people stopped caring, but because they got busy. We all got busy. So a lot of what I wanted to do with respect to my non-profit and how I wanted to reach and empower the masses of women had to be put on hold. But I never lost focus of my "push through" motto and I refused to give up because I HAD to reach them, to reach you all. So I had to find other avenues to spread my message of empowerment. And with every new idea that came, a renewed sense of self-doubt began that set in.

What about a blog? *No*, self-doubt said, *people will get tired of it or disinterested. Do you know how many blogs are already out there?* Ok. What about some speaking arrangements at other expos or women's conferences? *No, because you haven't been through enough to have a story anyone would want to listen to.* But don't we all have a story that needs to be told? *Yes, but your voice is so tiny that you'll never be able to stand in front of the crowd and be heard.* Ha! But look at God; won't He make a way?! Here I am, reaching the masses with the completion of this book. I have put my story out there, and I have started the spread of empowerment through my voice. It may not be on the platform I had once envisioned, but thousands will "hear" my voice through these pages and know my story in some manner. I have pushed through, and I found a way to be heard.

I say all of this to tell you about and introduce you to an underlying theme within these pages: make a way and never give up. There is a story in you that someone out there needs to hear. There is a talent in you that will only touch someone's life if you pursue that passion. There is a lesson that only you have uniquely experienced. However, it can still teach you how to help a fellow woman through a similar situation. After all, I have learned that life is not only about helping others pursue their passions- but also touching the lives of those that I come in contact with- and doing all I can to make a difference in this world, big or small, Because I Am Woman.

Do it anyhow!

In life, you'll be criticized for trying to achieve your goals. It may be a big venture which you are pursuing, a major passion of yours, or just a small feat you want to accomplish. There will be some people around to encourage you, but it is guaranteed that you will have haters lurking in the corners...do it anyhow!

You will be told by those closest to you that your dreams are too outlandish. They only know you for who you are right now. So, a big dream for you may seem too large of an accomplishment that they can't see you pulling off...do it anyhow!

You may be put down by those younger than you. They will tell you that you are way past your prime and that the task needs to be left to this new generation...do it anyhow!

You will hear from your own conscience that you're too young. From the lack of experience to not enough knowledge (just yet), you can become your own greatest critic. Don't listen to the self-doubt...do it anyhow!

You may feel intimidated by those with more experience. They have been doing what you want to do for years; drop those fears, ask them for advice and get some good pointers. Following in their footsteps can seem downright scary...do it anyhow!

People, doubts, and fears come with the territory of pursuing a passion or following your dreams. The anxiety of it all is a small factor. The obstacles may seem like big factors at first, but know this...you and God are the real big factors, and big outweighs the small, so...do it anyhow!

There's always room for growth.

Every day should be a learning experience, and we must not let a day go by without us learning more. Whether we are learning better ways to deal with others, i.e., colleagues or co-workers, to developing your talents, skills, and abilities, our minds should stay consistently open and we must soak up our environment like sponges. You would be amazed at the things you can learn just by actively paying attention and listening. When we learn, we grow, and our growth shows that we are living. Think in terms of plants, if they don't grow, that means they are what...dead, right? Right.

Furthermore, every aspect of your life has room for improvement. Whether it's your walk with God, your love for others, getting out of old habits, etc., no one is exempted from learning new things and growing oneself.

By improving our spiritual walk, we open our personal world up to the plans that God has for us. A lot of time God whispers the softest whisper, and if we don't have the proper relationship we may miss out on an opportunity to discern a spiritual calling He may have for us.

If we improve our love and respect for others, our days can go a lot smoother and lives a lot more peaceful. Letting go of grudges and past hurts, showing the right amount of love to our significant others and not leaving them guessing, or just showing those close to you that you care by performing kind gestures can improve relationships, and in the long run, develop your self-improvement.

Lastly, old habits can cause new destruction. Recognizing bad habits and vowing to improve your own ways to stop them is a great step. Hold yourself accountable.

And remember, whether you think of the cup as being half empty or half full, it doesn't matter. The point is that there's room for more.

Give and take should be 50/50, or else someone feels TAKEN advantage of.

Sometimes you give, sometimes you need, but never let the latter become more than the former.

We've all fallen on some kind of difficult time for one reason or another, and when you need help getting back on your feet, people in your corner step up and help you.

But don't be so needy that you drain the life and resources out of those that care for you, making them hesitant to offer help again. More importantly, don't let your time of need get you so down that you stop trying to do better for yourself or stop trying to pick yourself back up.

Think of it like this, soon someone may be depending on you for help, but how can you help them if you can't even help yourself. Keep a balance, and we can all depend on each other.

You've been challenged: Speak words of encouragement to at least three people this entire week.

Your mission, should you choose to accept...

You never know what others are going through. However, your simple words of encouragement may be something that someone needs to hear just in the nick of time. Life has a way of plummeting us with negative feelings. People have a way of bombarding us with negative vibes. Counter this negativity with positive words and send some encouragement toward someone's way. Your words might push them through to a breakthrough that they were close to.

I'll start it off here:
1) YOU are beautiful, inside and out!
2) YOU can do it!
3) YOUR smile brightens the world, use it more often!

How can someone else embrace you if YOU don't even embrace you?

They say, "How can you love someone else if you can't love yourself?" I say, "True that!"

When you walk in confidence, it is well and good, but anyone can put on a mask of assurance. Truly knowing your worth will exude an air about you and around you that 1) nobody can destroy and 2) that you will never doubt.

When the time comes for that one to sweep you off your feet, they won't have to worry about picking you up off the ground first.

The easy route isn't always best.

The easier thing to do isn't always the best thing to do. Giving up is easy, but anything worth getting has always come with a price. Sometimes, that price is hard work, while other times it is determination, focus, or even sacrifice. The question is, why give up when others, including yourself, are depending on you.

Stick it out, or try another way. Do what it takes to get through. It was never promised that the road would be easy, but the destination will be well worth it.

You weren't made to give up!

Think back on when you or someone you saw growing up was learning to crawl. You could barely hold your head up or even scoot, but you kept going until you did it though, didn't you? The same for walking; you fell so many times on your butt, maybe even cried a little, but it didn't stop you.

Science projects, dance moves, jump shots, even job applications, none of them probably came out perfect or yielded results at first, but look at you now. You learned what to do and what not to do, and now you are better for it.

Learn from mistakes, but never ever let what YOU think are failures stop you from going forward. There's a lesson in every misstep. Take it in stride, teach someone else what it taught you, but never let it stop you!

Be careful what you complain about.

There comes a time or two or fifty where we find ourselves upset, not feeling well, or just having a downright crappy day. It is very much in our human nature to complain about it to whoever willingly listens, and even someone that unwillingly listens. But keep in mind, your complaint might be the next woman's dream to experience.

Some women complain about the woes of pregnancy: swollen feet, the baby is dancing on her bladder, or she can no longer fit into her pre-maternity clothes. While she is complaining, or just simply venting, there is another woman out there who will never get the chance to experience those feelings due to infertility or has been longing for the chance to feel a baby grow in her womb, but her time has not come yet.

Other examples could be someone complaining about an unclean house, expensive oil changes, nagging boss, not taking into account the homeless, carless, jobless population(s) of women within earshot of these complaints. You never know the unintended damage it could be doing to their morale or ways of thought. Be mindful of your words. They say, "One man's trash is another man's treasure." I say, "One woman's grievance is another woman's goal."

Live in a way that you don't have to apologize for.

Mistakes happen. We're human, but don't go through life making promises that you will never keep and sound like a broken record of excuses.

If you tell your son/daughter that you'll be at the soccer game, do it. Make dinner plans with your significant other, go through with them. If the work was that important you would have been grinding all week to make it happen instead of cramming it into last minute frenzies and having to cancel on the more important things in life.

Moments of life are limited and precious moments are even rarer. So don't go around apologizing for not being there...just show up!

Poison is deadly.

I know, I know. You're saying, "Duhhhh." Lol. But hear me out.

Yes poison is harmful in the literal sense, but think of it outside of that context.

You have poisonous relationships, poisonous habits, poisonous views...and they all kill us softly, slowly, and sometimes swiftly. We have to learn to rid our lives of these poisonous and harmful things and allow more positive replacements. From friendships to how we take care of our finances, everything has an impact on our daily lives.

Take a look around you. Should the people, places, and things in your life be marked, "Danger! Hazardous materials?" Or do you just deal with them and continue wearing the uncomfortable "hazmat suit" of complacency?

Your reflections

We have all held onto something that should have been let go of a long time ago. Are you currently holding on to something? A person? An emotion? Junk? Rom toxic relationships to feelings of guilt or regret, what do you need to let go of? Reflect on it. What have you let go of that you need to give yourself credit for?

Reflect below.

_____
_____
_____
_____
_____
_____
_____
_____
_____
_____
_____
_____

JESSICA WOODRUFF

Let your past you be your only competition.

There's no need to compare your haves and have-nots to the next person. Just as there is no need in worrying what the next person is doing. Focus on you. What are you doing? What goals are you running after to make yourself better; to get you (and yours) out of that current complacent state of being?

What are you doing to build better relationships with those around you and the most important relationship, GOD?

How are you uplifting those needing it instead of bashing those that have what you're missing?

The only person you should be competing with is the person you're trying to be better than, and the only person you should be trying to be better than is the person you were yesterday.

Go get it. Period.

You are going to have someone in your ear telling you what you shouldn't do, and if you do it, how you should get it done. But most times, there will be at least one person at any given time throwing discouraging things your way. Don't take it so harshly, but you should take it to heart. Take it to heart and use it to show them that it can be done. Most of the time, the people telling you what you can't do are projecting their own lack of self-confidence onto you. They couldn't do it or don't think they can do it, so they tell you that you can't either.

#ByeFelicia! Don't let anything or anyone stop you. Use them to drive you, show them how it's done, and don't stop there...help them do it too! Maybe all they needed was a positive push to begin with.

Give without expectations.

Giving whole-heartedly means giving with your heart, not with your mind. When you start thinking about what you are giving, you then think about how the act will benefit you or what can the person receiving do for you. Sometimes you may give time, or money, or words. Yes, it is said give, and you shall receive, but what if all we are receiving is a happy feeling of doing well? I say, so what.

It's an added stress worrying about when you will receive your blessing for blessing others. Just know it will come and keep it moving. Enjoy that happy feeling you get at that moment.

Push through the pain and manifest in your purpose.

Heartbreak followed by setbacks. It seems to be the story of your life, and you're stuck in the movie, *Groundhog Day*. You can't see an end near, but never falter and definitely never give up. You could be closer than you think.

Pain is God's way of strengthening us; not only for our journey ahead, but to make us strong enough to help those coming behind us. Imagine pulling yourself out of a hole, and you barely made it because you were weak, but someone is following you out and needs a helping hand, but you can't lift them up because you're all tapped out. Are you just going to leave them there? No, you push through the feeling of sore, tired muscles, and pull the person out, too (or at least run and get help).

Our purpose in life is to not only fulfill our destiny but to help someone else achieve theirs as well. So, the next time the burden seems too heavy or it feels too hard to keep going, look to the heavens and say "Thank You, Lord, for strengthening me to help the next person out of their dungeon and into their destiny!" Fulfill that purpose of helping those around you reach their goals.

Not there yet? Surround yourself with those who are...no one will ever know the difference.

Surround yourself with 5 [insert whatever you want to be here], and you'll be the 6th.

Life is about connections and networking; if you know where you want to be and don't know how to get there, the best way to learn is from someone who has walked the walk.

Drop your pride or shy demeanor and go out there and find yourself a mentor. You'd be surprised at the number of people willing to disclose the secrets of the trade...maybe not exactly how they got to where they are (that might be best left unsaid. Lol), but taking in someone they can mentor is the way a good deal of people pay it forward.

Learn all you can, and when it's your time, remember the advice given and maybe avoid some of their costly mistakes. It could save you months, even years of time!

Show love and respect to your mother.

From the first moment you lay eyes on her, you know there's something special about this lady...something familiar, something that feels like home.

You discover quickly that she was given to you because she understands you; why you cry, when you hunger, or even when you need a diaper change.

You grow a little, and she's still there. Doctoring your scrapes, wiping your tears, and holding your hand. Time quickly passes, and the role doesn't change. She's still doctoring wounds and wiping tears, although this time from a broken heart or disappointment. Sympathetic eyes of untold "I told you so's," but still, the role never falters.

Mother. Mom. Mama. Mommie. Mum. Madre... whatever you call her, one day it just hits you why you were gifted such a wonderful woman. Why from day one she was all too familiar to you, and that's simply because she was meant for you, and you for her. To take care of each other and share love that only God can truly understand or match.

You may not have always seen eye to eye with her, but you will always see heart to heart. So, show love and respect to her. Everyone isn't as lucky as you to know a mother's love. Everyone isn't as lucky as you to still be able to give gifts and hugs. Whether it's just to pick up the phone or send a card in the mail, tell your mother (or a mother) that you love, honor, and respect her.

10 times out of 10, the only reason you CAN'T do something, involves one person: YOU!

Often times, our biggest limiting factors are our own limited thinking, our limited belief, and our limited drive. Plain and simple. Believing you can do something is a major part of the battle.

"I think I can, I think I can," isn't just a saying in a children's book. It should be a way of life. As a matter of fact, the words should be changed to "I know I can" And guess what, the most important part of that sentence is...I!

Believe in yourself; the rest will follow...including your skills and abilities, as well as other people's belief in you, too.

Passion with no plan won't get you to your purpose.

This saying reminds me of when teachers would tell you to write out an outline for a paper, project, etc. in order to make the actual process go a bit smoother. An outline is probably one of the only things learned that we could take into our adult life and use (Pythagorean Theorem, who?).

You can't go blindly into trying to fulfill your dreams and expect to just get there. Sometimes you have to map out your next moves, analyze your next steps, and contemplate your next position.

From figuring out who has done it before you, and how...to the cost(s) and sacrifices needed...to the projected time (although we are all on God's time, maybe you are going back to school for a certification, how long will it take?)...to the help you may need (and figuring out the right words to say to butter the right folks up lol).

An outlined plan could not only make steps easier but can help you stay focused as well. Some things won't just fall in your lap or into place, so you have to map out a path to your purpose.

Rejection= Redirection

Don't get mad, get even and prove whoever told you "No," that they were wrong. Prove anyone that ever doubted you wrong. Don't get mad, keep pushing. Push past that failed attempt at greatness. Guess what...you're getting a second chance at it. Use it to your advantage by learning from your mistakes, looking past that roadblock, and moving on.

Sometimes a new direction is needed in life. And sometimes, it's with that new direction that we find our peace, our joy, and our truly intended purpose.

Always remain genuine and true. Love people for who they are, not for what they can do [for you].

Our society has become such a 'what have you done for me lately' type of place that the norm is to only keep people around that benefit us in some way. Oh, he cuts my grass when I need it, let me be nice. She watches my children at the drop of a hat, let me be nice. But when was the last time you did something or were nice to someone that could never repay you?

Stop looking at people only as benefactors and really see them for who they are. Yes, it's great to have help in your corner, but give help more than you look to get help. It could make a world of difference.

Your reflections

Have any of the passages stuck out to you so far? Do you find yourself competing with others when you should just focus your energy on your own life's endeavors? Have you been rejected by someone or denied an opportunity, only to realize it was for your own good?

Reflect below.

_____
_____
_____
_____
_____
_____
_____
_____
_____
_____
_____
_____
_____

JESSICA WOODRUFF

Good or bad, you magnify what you focus on.

Focus on greatness, bring about great things. You want to perpetuate negativity, concentrate on that. Whatever you focus more energy on is what will come about the most profound in your life. Pay close attention to what you give close attention to.

Magnify the awesomeness that you want to manifest in your life. Think of only positive thoughts, feelings, and emotions. Watch the change for the better in you.

Second chances save you.

God is the God of second chances, we know it all too well, right? We also know that He wants us to be more like Him, and walk in His image, so why is it so hard for us to give second chances?

Not only does forgiveness take a load off of us, but it releases the burden and stress associated with holding that grudge. Stress is definitely a leading factor of many ailments. So in forgiving, not only are we saving ourselves in the eternal aspect ("forgive, and it shall be forgiven unto you." Lol), but we save ourselves in the short run, too. Make sense? Try it out and watch the difference it makes in your life.

You give your fears so much energy, why not invest that into your dreams?

Imagine a world where we truly let go and let God. A world where we just cast all fears, worries, doubts, or whatever aside and truly chased after our dreams. Not only chase them but capture them and put them on our mantle. Lol. Oh what a world it would be.

Now, what's stopping you from doing just that? If you're scared, say you're scared, but just as you opened your mouth to confess it, open your mouth to cast out that spirit of fear as well.

{2 Timothy 1:7 Look it up. Marinate on it.}

Don't put your life on hold for someone who hits the ignore button on you.

Sometimes we are so quick to jump up and be at someone else's beck and call that we don't pay attention to their response to us when we ask for a favor. Sacrificing all of your time for someone who won't even lift a finger to help you stops now!

Often times we focus so much on the love and affection we have that spills out to others that we totally miss that they aren't reciprocating the actions. Giving your all to someone who won't even loan you a piece of their attention stops now!

Know your worth and know that you're worth more than being put on the back burner to be kept "warm" (content) for them to pay attention to you at their convenience. Believe that.

Sometimes you just need a minute.

I'm not really sure where we get the notion of feeling guilty for taking time out for ourselves. Yes, we do family vacations and communal relaxation, but ask yourself, when was the last time you really took a moment for you?

Just pack an overnight or weekend bag, check into a hotel where nobody knows your name...no kid access, the Boo knows to only call in dire emergencies, and even then he or she knows how to dial 911. Lol.

But seriously, everyone, and I mean everyone, from Oprah to the POTUS and FLOTUS, needs a recharge. So go ahead and book that room, spa day, or whatever you need and carry around a "Do Not Disturb" sign and chill-ax. You can even take turns with your spouse. Haha! Either way, you deserve it.

#TakingMyOwnAdvice.

Nobody's perfect, but you're perfect for me.
−God

    We often times want to wait to go to God when we feel worthy of Him...thinking He won't accept us for who we are. I'm here to tell you, He loves you, flaws and all.

    When you met your boo thang, were you perfect? No, but you surely pretended to be right? Ha! The wonderful thing about my God is that He accepts you how you are, no flexing needed. He loves the broken, damaged, and lost. He favors the ones He can do the most work on and through. Can you imagine the glory He can receive from your testimony of "starting from the bottom now you here?" He's in love with you regardless of your past and present, so let Him in. Remember, He sent His only son to die for your sins, our sins; that's how much He loves us. Perfect or not, you're His boo. Take advantage of the wonders of Him.

There's nothing wrong with talking to yourself, as long as it's positive affirmations (or saying "put down the cookie." Lol)

With so much negative talk happening on the outside, we need some positive reinforcements in our lives.

Talk to yourself. Boost yourself. Sometimes, all we have to say to ourselves is, "Kudos, job well done." Besides, nobody spends as much time with you as you do, so be a positive influence on yourself.

Today, tell someone 'Thank you!'

Sometimes, life hits us hard, and it may have us feeling like we can't get anything right. Imagine the days where you work your butt off, maybe for yourself or maybe for someone else; you could have been at work, or you could have been planning and executing a party for your teenager; just think of that time and imagine if no one told you thank you for your hard work. How would it have made you feel? Maybe they did fail to tell you thanks…how did it make you feel?

Feeling appreciated not only helps us feel good about our works, but it also helps encourage us to continue to do good things for people or to continue our hard work. So, if you want people to keep doing favors for you, you better start opening your mouth and telling them 'thanks.'

You don't even have to study the scale to know that positive always outweighs the negative.

The good will surely happen and so will the bad. But one thing about it is that focusing on the bad won't make the good that happened just go away; just like focusing on the good won't take away the bad that happened. But you know what, I bet looking to the good will have a much more profound effect than if you only focus on the bad.

Joy comes from positivity. Peace comes from positivity. Life comes from positivity, and so does growth. So grow from the lessons you learned in the bad times. Smile at the lessons you learned in the good times. Whatever you do, know that good always overpowers and outweighs bad.

Open your door...let OUT the hurt and let IN happiness.

Sometimes, we all need to do some deep spring cleaning in our homes, cars, and offices.

But how many of us actually do a cleansing of our lives? We open up the windows and doors on that first crisp spring weathered day and let out the dank of winter, letting in a refreshing, renewing breeze. But what's so different with our lives?

Plug in the metaphor into your world. Evaluate the old, invite in the new. Seasons change, and sometimes it's time to change our surroundings, from places to things to even people. Change can bring about peace, if we let out the bad and let in the good.

To me, spring represents a new beginning. Maybe it's time for a new beginning in your life...

The road may be bumpy, but the destination will be breathtaking!

Flat tires, low gas, all the potholes in life and not one of these should be able to rob you of getting to that great destination of yours. You have somewhere to be, and so many people are depending on you and waiting on you to get there. Don't let a season of not so smooth roads put a halt on your journey. Those days just build character and make the final destination that much more with it!

You don't have the right to stop being epic just because the next person doesn't see it.

I've said it before, and I will say it a million times...you don't need another person to validate your awesomeness. Stop looking for approval from the next person. You were created in His image and of the likes of Him, and my God is definitely awesome. Therefore, if God says it's so, then it is so. He's all you need in your corner. And I'm just here to make sure that you don't ever forget that!

BECAUSE I AM WOMAN: *Reflections of a Woman*

Your reflections

Sometimes we let the opinions of others hold us back from so much of the potential we have inside. Sometimes we can't be great, not because the next person doesn't see it, but because we can't see it in ourselves. Look at your reflection in the mirror. What do you need to hear? What are you good at? What phenomenal things can you do with the limitless power you hold? What can you say to yourself to get you to believe it?

Reflect below.

_____
_____
_____
_____
_____
_____
_____
_____
_____
_____
_____
_____
_____

Don't ask for the blessing if you're not willing to put the work in for it.

I found myself guilty of this, but not anymore. I realized that if I want something, I had to hit the ground running and make moves. God will clear paths, hand you tools, and even whisper your next step to you. However, he will not pick up the controller and move your right foot, then left foot, the right foot again to get you to your destination. Nope boo. If you don't work, you don't eat. No point in praying for rain when you haven't even plowed the field or sowed the seeds.

Sometimes you have to take a step back in order to move forward.

Life moves fast, and sometimes decisions have to be made on a whim. But do you ever really take a step back from your situation and look at all options before jumping to that conclusion?

Probably not, because life moves fast. Lol. But remember, life is like chess...your next move can have an adverse effect on the outcome of the game. It's ok to take a second to stop and scope out all options, then make the move. And while you're at it, it wouldn't hurt to throw a prayer or two in the mix.

Dust yourself off and try again!

It may take multiple avenues to get to your final destination. If the boat sinks, jump on the plane; if the plane crashes, jump in the car. However, never, ever give up because that method didn't get you to where you need to be.

It's like stopping after the first "No" from a bank. Or worrying about someone saying, "Weren't you that phonograph guy? Now you're doing electricity? When are you going to give it up?" (Look up Thomas Edison).

Let them wonder, but don't let it stop you. Rock your dream 'til the wheels fall off, and even after that it will be so well polished that you will slide to your goal! Just don't give up!

Are you more obsessed with your past or your potential?

We focus so much on what we've been through or even what we've done, that we discount ourselves with respect to where we are going. Even God is willing to overlook your past transgressions when you ask Him for forgiveness, so why can't we stop focusing so much on our own mistakes?

Your past may have shaped your life, but it doesn't have to determine who/what you ARE. You are out of your past, meaning that was not the destiny for you. Keep it moving; you have somewhere to be!!

You're not being punished, you're being pushed.

I have to continually tell myself this; God did not design you for ordinary. He did not design you for average. He didn't even design you for good. You are meant to be great. He wants you to excel. He wants the absolute best for you, and if that involves literally knocking the mediocre out of your life or your hands so you can open up and receive the phenomenal blessings He has coming your way, then He has no problem doing that.

So when you mope and moan about something not going as planned or this path you are currently on just seems to keep leading to disappointments, and thinking like each failure you face is a reprimand, just know that God is plunging and purging you out of complacency. Go be purged!

Don't cling to a mistake just because you spent a lot of time making it. -Unknown

Now, this rings true for any mishap in life; relationships, jobs, or even friendships. My goodness! How many of you just hold on just because of the longevity of the situation. Shaking my head at me. Shaking my head at you. Lol. But if it's time to let go, that's what you have to do. It's like a tug-of-war with giants...no point in holding on and getting rope burn if you know you're going to lose anyway.

People can be draining. Don't give your energy to anyone that doesn't deserve it.

Boy oh boy! Whether it's a Negative Nancy yapping in your ear, or someone who you continue to entertain that had you stuck on the same channel you should have turned from a long time ago, people will suck the life right out of you if you let them. It's like the more you listen to them, the more they can power up their negativity or the more energy they get for playing games with you.

Learn that if you let people drain you of your energy, you won't be able to keep any for yourself to tackle more pressing issues that need your attention. Unplug from them. You'll be a better you!

You might not feel like it, but you don't have to walk around looking like you don't feel like it.

I feel like this is the perfect Monday excerpt. So, if you get to this page and it is not Monday, either wait or imagine it is. Lol!

(•••••••••••••holding••••••••••••)

I know we all had a "case of the Mondays" today as we started off our work week, but I hope nobody walked around with a permanent scowl on their face. Nothing worse than that 'unapproachable look,' especially as women. Not only do we have to put on a happy face when things aren't all that happy, but in the home life, there is absolutely no such thing as I don't feel like it. The babies don't know what that means! They need feeding, homework needs proof-reading, butts need bathing; and if we don't do it, who will? (No offense guys. Lol.)

So anytime you just don't feel like it, do it anyway. Imagine if all the great leaders before us never did it because they didn't feel like it. Where would we be today?

You can't stumble upon anything while sitting down.

A common theme in this book seems to be getting up and doing something. The simple notion of taking a small first step puts you eons ahead of the 'you' that doesn't do anything.

I don't know what goal(s) you have set for yourself, but take an initial step to start making it happen. Whether the goal is to start a business, change careers, buy a home, etc.; see if you can't network with individuals that already have knowledge of what it is you want to do. Google it, YouTube it, hop on LinkedIn, whatever. But you won't find that jackpot of a next step sitting on your...sofa.

It's your turn, so make your move.

He's waiting on you to make your move, it shouldn't be the other way around. We sit around waiting on God to fulfill our dreams for us and when it doesn't come to fruition, we think it wasn't meant to be. No. If you want something, go out and get it. THEN He will place all of the persons, places, and things on the path that you need to succeed.

Your reflections

Think about a time that you were waiting on God. You may have prayed for signs or prayed for Him to make a divine move in your life. Did He come through? Did you have to take a step first and then you started to see results take place? What happened? Details, sis!

Reflect below.

_____
_____
_____
_____
_____
_____
_____
_____
_____
_____
_____
_____

JESSICA WOODRUFF

Surround yourself with people that will push you to be greater.

We all need a support system, but nobody needs a support system that is full of complacent, average, or stagnant people.

We have to surround ourselves with people that not only want to see us move forward, but will also give us the shove to keep going when we doubt ourselves or feel like quitting. In turn, we have to do that for them, too.

Team work makes the dream work; why not push others to reach their goals while they push you as well? If someone is losing sight of their goal or their grip is slipping from their dream, pull them up!

Don't treat him like a king if he is acting like a joker!

Ladies, ladies, ladies!!

We are so quick to take what we can get these days. Don't reduce your standards for someone that is merely entertaining to you if he is not here being uplifting, treating you with the utmost respect, or pushing you to be a better you.

We have to wise up. You cannot expect to be treated like a queen by anyone other than your equal. Royalty recognizes royalty. Be a queen without being played like a deck of cards.

Instead of asking 'why is this happening TO ME'...you should be asking 'why is this happening FOR ME?'

We can so easily complain about events that occur in our life that we see as unfortunate, and cry out in anguish, "Why me, Lord?"

But what if we ever took the time to look at our situations and see that God has a plan in ALL THINGS: good, bad, ugly, and pretty. Analyze before you assume. God sometimes sends us through trials to mold us into the person we are supposed to be. So maybe the trial isn't happening TO bring you down, but instead FOR the betterment of you as a person. Try to change your views on circumstances; your life will be better for it.

Choose your words wisely. You determine your highs and lows for the day.

It sounds cheesy when people tell you to wake up in the morning, look in the mirror, and say, "It's going to be a great day!"

This may be true, but cheesy or not, it's better than waking up out of bed and complaining about everything under the sun. Or even worse, claiming; "this is going to be a long day" or, "can this day get any worse?" when a few things don't go your way. I don't encourage this due to repercussions on your part (lol), but if you're brave enough try waking up to negative thoughts for a week, then to positive for a week...see which week is better. It is guaranteed that the positive week will be better. Besides, who cares if it is cheesy...nobody will see you doing it but you.

Your circumstances are pushing back to make you stronger.

We have those days or times where life comes at us hard. There's no denying it and no need to front because God sends "rain on the just and the unjust," but know it all happens for a reason.

When you are putting in work at the gym or lifting weights, it's not easy, but the resistance builds muscle. The same goes for tough events and hard circumstances. They test your strength, but also make you stronger...stronger in faith of God, yourself, and those around you, if applicable (lol).

So when life pushes you, push back with a belief in your heart that you can make it no matter what. (We weren't given Philippians 4:13 for no reason)

Last year you said "Next month." Last month you said "Tomorrow." You ready yet?

If I'm not talking to myself on this page...boy I tell ya!

We seem to put off a lot of important things on our to-do list. It is either work or fun gets in the way, or doing for others gets in the way. What if we put it off for too long? If we never get to complete that to-do list?

Lives that were supposed to be changed will never be changed. Souls that were lost might remain that way. The light you were called to be, flickers out before you could light the next torch. What if?

I say this to say slow progress is still progress. Write a page of that book each week if you have to. Get the business plan written down AT LEAST. If you know someone that does what you have a passion for, reach out to them. Just do something! The world's waiting on YOU!

Failure comes from doing, but so does success. Either way, it's on you to make a move.

We would never know we could if we never tried. We would never see success if we never took that first step. We could never be the change we want to see if we don't first be the change. Progress will never happen if we are stagnant. Success is the result of an action, not the outcome of merely dreaming. If we don't make a move, the momentum is never created, and evolvement can never happen. Just start.

God has a funny way of preparing you for greater...so laugh!

Often times, we may find ourselves asking, "Why me?"

Going through certain things can be a hard pill to swallow, but I say why not us? Why not get the opportunity to show non-believers the grace our Father shows us daily, the favor that rests upon our lives, the way our faith in Him can keep us going through even the toughest times, or that we know He is getting us ready for greater with every trial that is thrown our way.

God has His way of testing our strength and building character. So stop complaining about your current situation. You asked for this moment the second you prayed for an upgrade.

Tattered sails from the rough seas become irrelevant when you make it to shore.

Imagine a long trip you have had to take. Day turned into night, or night into day, depending on what time you started out. You hit some bumps along the way, possibly a flat tire. Bugs splattered on your windshield. Restroom breaks or stretch stops seemingly prolong the travel. When you finally reach that destination, isn't it a huge breath of fresh air? Wasn't it worth all the hassle?

No matter what you go through in life, know that once you reach that end-goal, all of the hardships, obstacles, and hiccups will be just something to look back on and say, "I made it through," when you reach your purpose.

It's difficult (if not impossible) to go into new heights being the old you.

Yes indeed. New blessings sometimes call for new surroundings: 1) because not everyone will be happy for you, and 2) because you can't take everybody with you to your new destination...including who you used to be. So leave what's supposed to be left in the past there...meaning your old attitude, your old way of thinking, and old habits. New levels already equate new devils, so why bring along the old ones too?

If you can't congratulate, don't open your mouth to criticize.

It's so easy to find the faults in others; be it their actions, mannerisms, habits, looks, etc. We can go all day long listing what we don't like about someone or what we don't like about what they do. However, how often do we sit back and say to ourselves or even express openly how proud we are of an individual's (individuals') accomplishment(s), goals they set and met, or how good they have done? I know with some people it's hard, but accept the challenge. Someone might need to hear a little positive remark.

Opposition leads to a new position.

Sit back sometimes and notice how it seems every time you run into issues, problems, or whatever, that soon after the best thing in life seems to happen.

You got fired from your job, but as soon as you start to get down and out about it, you get a phone call for the interview you've been waiting on for months. Higher paying job, same exact work, if not less.

Passed up for that promotion that you thought you wanted, only to get another position beyond your wildest dreams.

The house you knew was perfect for your family fell through, but the one you actually close on has more rooms, a bigger backyard, and a cheaper mortgage payment.

Don't always look at opposition as an obstacle. Sometimes God is giving you time to prep yourself for the greater that He has prepared. Trust Him.

Your reflections

Have you ever been in a position where it seemed like nothing was going how you planned, and just when you were ready to pout about it, something amazing ended up happening instead? What "blocked blessings" have you complained about only to get "double for your trouble" later on?

Reflect below.

_____
_____
_____
_____
_____
_____
_____
_____
_____
_____
_____
_____
_____

Seasons change, but you can't be afraid to embrace what's new.

We sometimes get overwhelmed with change and the 'new us.' People long for the good old days when there were less creaks and cracks coming from the bones. Even wishing for that high school body... 21-year-old body... 30-year-old body.

We have to learn to love where we are now, who we are now, and even the struggles we endured to get here.

Think of a beautiful butterfly. It used to be a cute little caterpillar. Life hit it and stuck it in a cocoon, but it emerged with gorgeous wings. How does that butterfly go back to being a caterpillar? Technically it can't, but in fantasy it would have to get rid of what makes it marvelous.

Love yourself. Embrace the new you. Someone out there thinks those grays and wrinkles are sexy.

Take time for YOU.

This can't be stressed enough. It's in no way being selfish. I like to call it "burnout prevention."

Being overworked, overstressed, and over-tired is very bad for you and those around you. Not only are you risking burnout, where you definitely won't be able to help anyone/do anything for anyone, but your attitude, health, and task performance are all affected. Nobody can concentrate or function running on 'E.'

Taking time out for you can help eliminate all of this. Whether it's a vacation or a quiet bubble bath, do it. Your mind, body, and soul will definitely thank you for it.

Never forget, God is greater.

We have seasons of life where nothing seems to go OUR way. Cut backs on the jobs. Negative bank accounts. Lost friendships. Failed relationships. We just can't seem to find light at the end of the tunnel, the never ending tunnel. But hasn't something like this happened before? Didn't we make it through and live to tell about it? Didn't it bring us closer to our Lord and savior? Or is that just me?

No matter what problems you may face, dilemmas you may encounter, or circumstances you may run into, always remember there is always one who is bigger than any obstacle you may come across that can pick you up and place you on the other side of victory! Even in the darkest hours, God will never leave us or forget us; so don't forget His power over your life.

Don't count yourself out and then wonder why others won't count on you.

This has been especially true to me since I have been an entrepreneur. I have found that people flock to those who have confidence. Confidence in one's self, confidence in their knowledge of self, and confidence in their product or brand.

If you are trying to sell yourself, but don't believe in YOU, neither will anyone else. I don't know about you, but if someone comes to me sounding like they're a 3 year old giving an Easter speech, I will think twice. Lol!

Believe in yourself. It can take you far!

Make it a point in your day to let someone know that they matter.

Sometimes all it takes is a quick phone call or a " Thinking about you..." text that could mean the world to someone.

You'd be surprised what might brighten up a person's day or week. Reach out to friends and family. If you know they were working on a new project or started a new job, ask them how the transition is going. Small things add up!

Pray on it, but don't stay on it.

    Being indecisive on huge decisions is not only costly to you, but also costly to the future you. Trying to move on, but holding on to things of the past will do more harm than good. If it is meant for you to take it into your new beginning, it will come easy. If it's not meant to be, it could be pulling you back/down into detrimental circumstances.

    Pray on it, but don't stay on it. It can be hard to move on sometimes, but you may end up worse off playing Double-Dutch with what was and what should be.

The easiest way to get over your past is to LEAVE IT THERE!

Don't spend your days thinking of what "coulda," "shoulda," or "woulda" been. Because if it "shoulda" been, it would be and if it "coulda" been, it can be.

God places things and people in our lives for a reason, and he removes things and people for a reason as well. We just have to trust Him with what was and what shall be.

If the time has passed, just let it be. So much heartache comes from people thinking they can be time travelers. Leave the past alone. It is probably gone for a reason.

Your struggle wasn't meant to define you; it simply molds you into who you are.

We have to be careful how we label ourselves and the people we love. Don't say things like, "she's an alcoholic," but instead say she is dealing with alcoholism. That can also be said for depression, drug addictions, etc.

People want to be SOMETHING or be defined as something so bad that they tend to take those titles and hold onto them simply because it's a title. And when it's time to get better, do better, and be better, they hesitate because they've held onto that title so long that it has become who they think they are and they don't want to lose their identity...so they remain stuck.

Just think before you label.

There is no reward in tearing someone down.

Not too much to elaborate about on this one folks. All I can say is if ever you are feeling like speaking ill of someone else behind their back, try replacing those thoughts with something positive to say in their face, or someone else's face. Give a compliment, give credit where it's due, but just don't give the world negative vibes. There's enough out there already.

Besides, have you ever swung a hammer to nail something? How about a sledge hammer to tear down a wall? Which was easier? The small hammer (compliment) was far easier to swing than the sledge hammer (destructive words). In other words, building up is easier than tearing down, in this case.

Just because someone doesn't see it, doesn't mean you aren't worth it.

You got passed up for the job you were interviewed for. So what? Didn't make the team? Ok. He left you after you gave your all. Big deal. Not to sound harsh, but everything happens for a reason. When one door closes, well, you know the rest.

Sometimes, things happen, and we focus so much on "what" happened that we forget to pay attention to "why" it happened. There's always a lesson, and there's always something greater after. Don't let a small worry validate your big worth.

If you're still breathing, you are here for a reason. #Purpose

Think back on someone you know that has gone before you. Did they touch your life? Did they make a difference in the community?

Now take a long look at your life. Are you making a difference in someone else's life...a positive impact? What have you done for someone that could never repay you?

Every day that we wake up is God's way of telling us that our job isn't quite done yet. It's a new day to fulfill a dream. A new day to make a difference. Show Him that you are indeed grateful for another chance, and do something.

Some won't understand. They weren't meant to.

You decided to walk away from a job you've been at for decades. People ask why. A long-time relationship or friendship ends. More inquiries.

No matter what you do, there will always be someone asking you why you did it or telling you that you shouldn't have done it. But let's get one thing clear...what's for you is for you and what's not is not. And nobody else HAS to know your reasons behind it besides you and God. This is because in the end, you will be the one dealing with your decisions, and He will be the one you answer to.

Your success depends on YOU.

The only valid thing success contains is "U." Not he, she, or them. It's up to you. True, you need help and guidance along the way, but essentially YOUR success is determined by the blood, sweat, and tears YOU put into your endeavors.

Now look at the word successful...it has two u's...representing the two you's that you will encounter. One 'you' gets you to your breaking point, and the other 'you' pushes you forward and says, "I got this!"

You are what you say you are.

Speaking positivity over your life is important, but so is speaking positivity into yourself. I had to catch myself on this a few times, and I'm still working on it. The top one people use... "Whew, I'm so broke..." Or "Ugh! I'm so fat..."

Speak life into yourself. "I may not be able to get this now, but when I'm wealthy..." Claim it! "When I lose some pounds..." "When I undergo more personal development..."

You'll be amazed how your life and circumstances change when you are more positive about how you view yourself.

Your reflections

Words are more powerful than we think. What negative thoughts have you old yourself in the past? Don't write them down below; instead, for every negative thought, write a positive affirmation in its place. After you have written them, read them again out loud.

Reflect below.

_____
_____
_____
_____
_____
_____
_____
_____
_____
_____
_____
_____
_____

The only time the words "I CAN'T" should be used is if they precede the words "WITHOUT GOD."

Believing in yourself is one thing...believing in the power of God is another. They must, however, go hand in hand. We put goals in our minds and desires in our hearts and when we can't get them accomplished, we give up. Therein lies the problem. When you rely on you, you can fail easily. , but when you seek the help of God, you can do ALL things. He supplies the strength, endurance, and confidence. The only thing you have to do is move when He calls you.

The prelude to your life's story should always be an attitude of gratitude.

"Thank you in advance" is one way we sign off on a letter. Why is that? It is because we have hope and expectancy for whatever request we made in the letter. Correct? Not only are we hoping for something in lieu of sending the letter, we also show appreciation for the person's time which he or she is taking to even read the letter and whatever inconvenience the request may cause.

Life should be no different. Every day God is waking you up and working out things in your life that will be for your good. We should not only thank/praise Him in advance for what we ask of Him but before we even fix our mouths to make another request, we should be thanking Him for what He has already done for us. He didn't have to, but He did it anyhow. We weren't deserving, but He did it anyhow. And we thank You in advance for your time.

{ }

Sometimes, you just have no words. Sometimes you feel like your words will go unheard. Sometimes silence speaks louder than words, and sometimes you feel all three situations apply. It is ok when you don't have the words. It is ok when you feel like they should be kept to yourself. We try so hard to be heard, to get our points across, to get someone to LISTEN. Sometimes, silence speaks louder, and it is ok.

In ALL things we must give THANKS.

Give thanks for all that you have, and all that you are. But don't forget to give thanks for the potential things as well.

If you have a family that you are able to spend time with, be thankful. If you have a family, but you all just don't get along, be thankful. Not for the strife in your relationships, but in the opportunity God has given you to see another day to make things right. Some people will never get that chance.

The same can go for a job you have, but aren't completely pleased with. What can you do to change it? Be grateful for the opportunity as you look for something that better suits you. In the case of your house, you may not be in that dream house you've always wanted, but be thankful for a new day to change that situation, too.

There is power in the potential that can take you far, and each new day can potentially be what you perceive as your worst, or potentially be the best. In all of it, thank God for the opportunity.

Why not now?

How many times (in a day) do we say, "I'll handle it later," or "I'll get to that tomorrow"? I am starting to think tomorrow is an imaginary concept because in a lot of dealings, it never comes.

Not only do we put off work assignments, chores, and other small dealings, but we often times put our God assignments off, too. That book you were going to write later, which never came. The business you were going to start, perfect conditions never happened.

How long shall we make the excuse called "later"?

Procrastination is a prosperity killer. Make an effort to stop delaying your duties. You could be delaying something that could serve as a blessing to others; and for all we know, tomorrow may never come.

Count your blessings (and don't get upset when you run out of fingers).

  We sometimes forget to count the "small" things that we take for granted. Running water, shoes, a car that may not have air conditioning, but it works and so do the windows. If we count, on a daily basis, the things we should be grateful for, we may find it exhausting saying "thank You, God," by the end of the day.
  Well, you'd better get to it.

Your failures should give you a green light, not a stop sign.

Remember learning to ride your bike and all of the times you fell before you could even get a good push off? Yeah, me too. But you didn't stop because you messed up, you kept going, right?

I wonder where we stopped letting the mess ups push us harder and started letting failures tell us, "No we can't."

Maybe it was when we got reprimanded for our bad grades or demoted because we missed a deadline at work. Who knows? What I do know is that we have to get out of those elementary ways and let what we think we failed at push us to greater heights. When you mess up, keep going. Find better ways to do it, perfect the ways you were taught, but never, ever quit. That's for suckers!

Happy is a personal emotion.

Happiness is what YOU make it. What makes you happy may not be for someone else, and vice versa. And you know what? The beauty in that is, no one can take it from you unless you let them.

So with that being said, do what brings joy to you, be who brings joy to you, and hold on to it for dear life.

God does not accept resignation letters.

Don't think that just because you have been divinely given a purpose that it will be an easy feat. God gives us the script and allows us to play the lead role, but He wants to make sure that we know He is still the writer, director, and producer. When the stunts get hard, it's not time to give up. It's time to look to Him for direction. That's all He wants from us...to lean on Him in troubled times, not throw in the towel. It's ok to throw your hands up, as long as they are outstretched to Him!

Haters will probably never congratulate you, but your success will definitely keep them on their toes.

 I have seen it often on my journey to fulfill my purpose...when you accomplish a goal you set out to achieve, you will have those people watching you that just refuse to give you credit for making it. One thing they may do, though, is go back in attempts to accomplish something of their own. You write a book; they want to write one now. You have a clothing line; they want to design fashion, too.
 Keep winning; that way you can keep them too busy trying to emulate you that they won't have time to throw real shade.

Believing the sun is behind the clouds is fine; knowing it will shine again is what gets you through.

I can believe in God all day long, but it's my faith in Him that keeps me going…the faith that He can and will make a way out of no way. The faith that with Him I can move mountains. The faith that through every trial and tribulation I will come out victorious because it is in His word. Just because someone believes He exists doesn't mean they believe He will provide, heal, comfort, or be whatever it is that we need. Belief is only half the battle.

Live on purpose.

You go to work with a set goal in mind: get sales up, increase customer base, or make the boss happy. You go to the grocery store for set reasons: get the food on this list, kids need snacks, and stay within the food budget.

So why don't we live our real lives this way? Set personal goals that you can attain, make budgets, make a to-do list or even a bucket list. But don't go through life wandering (or wondering) aimlessly. Live for a cause, make a difference in yourself and for yourself, and use that resolve to uplift others around you.

Your reflections

What short-term, long-term, and in-between goals have you set for yourself? Do you have any goals that involve other people, i.e. hang out with your friends once a month or eat together as a family more often?

Reflect below.

Change is a process, not an overnight miracle.

Another downfall in this fast-paced world is that we want everything instantly. From microwaved meals to ten-minute oil changes and even grits! Lol.

But have you ever noticed that the longer something takes, the better it tastes or looks? Slowly cooked beans seem to taste better. Losing weight the longer way gives you time to better-tone, lose excess skin, and is easier to keep off pounds.

We want to see results so instantaneously that we forget to enjoy the ride along the way, take in the scenery, and learn from the smaller lessons on the journey.

If you keep at it long enough you will see the difference...might not be a next day thing but have patience with yourself, and don't give up!!

Learn to discern what you yearn.

Ha! I thought that was pretty clever. Lol...any who...

So many life decisions have come from impulse moves while in a bind or in the excitement of the moment. But know this, if you take some time to pray before you act on it, it can save you a lot of heartache and headache (sssss).

I'm not saying you should give up on your dream if it's taking a while for it to come to fruition. No. But is that dream of yours God's desire and plan for your life? Sit down, ask Him, and wait for His answer. If it is in fact no, wait for what He has in store for you. I promise it's something far greater.

Feed your spirit with positive energy.

Not much to say on this one, besides try it out. See how good you'll feel on the inside and watch the shift in the atmosphere around you as you drive out negative thoughts, feelings, and emotions.

Sometimes you have to look fear in the eye and spit in its face.

Declare that you will no longer be a scaredy cat. Declare that you will take the first step to do what you need to do to be who you need to be. Declare that even if I am down right now, I can get back up.

Yes, spitting is un-lady like and disrespectful, but fear has disrespected you long enough. It has kept you afraid to live out your dreams; kept you afraid to try something different; and even kept you afraid to try again. But no more. Not now, not ever again!

Enjoy the little things.

With such busy lifestyles we oftentimes forget to stop and smell the roses, so to speak.

Working on a promotion and we fail almost always to work on our health. Trying to make partner at the firm and we forget about our child's championship game.

Sometimes we just have to slow down. Crunch some fall leaves like you used to love to do. Catch a 'lightning bug' in a jar. But most of all, spend some time with the people that matter most.

Life is full of small, precious moments...you'll miss out on the small ones always trying to create HUGE moments for yourself.

Don't let your opinion of others' opinion of you stop you from success.

Oftentimes we hesitate on doing what we want to do because we worry about how other people would react. STOP IT!!

Whether you are up or whether you are down, someone will always have something to say. Use that talk as motivation to keep going. You're obviously making headlines in their world, do something spectacular so they'll eventually only be able to say, "Wow! They really did it."

Persistence is the key.

Diligence is a sure way to get the outcome you are going for. If you are diligent at sitting around doing nothing, your results will be just that. If you diligently put in work, effort, etc. you will soon see the fruits of your labor come to pass. What you put in, you get out; what you don't put in, well...you know how that goes.

Be content, but stay away from complacency.

It's ok to be happy where you are...grateful even, but life gets you down when you settle for less than greatness. People are meant to move...staying still makes you stiff. Sometimes, we get so comfortable where we are, that we forget that we need to be doing something else, i.e., sitting on a comfy couch, knowing we need to take care of the laundry or dishes. The same goes for sitting at the same job for 20 years because we are so used to it, when we know for certain that there is something greater out there for us to be doing and pursuing. So, be happy with where you are, but don't stop moving forward to get to your greater destination, to be your greater self.

No more excuses.

Always remember, someone is counting on you to reach your goals and live out your dreams. It may not be your direct offspring, they may not be related to you at all. However, something positive that you accomplish can benefit others for generations to come.

Think of those that came before you. Now imagine if they had given up. Your reason to keep going is far greater than your reason to quit. Don't lose sight of it! Don't give yourself a reason to let YOU down.

Be contagious.

    Thought I'd mess with your mind today.
    With all the drama of the world; social media and regular media spreading news like wildfire...who will keep the peace?
    You can! Be infectious with your joy, your peace, your love, your compassion. Somebody may be looking to something/someone for aspiration...be the light they need...be the beacon of hope and spread it to all.

The devil is a lie!

In the brink of chaos, and you feel like you're one of the few remaining calm?

Don't allow others to make you feel crazy because you know the promises of your Father. Also, after brushing off the crazy feelings, don't let the devil get in your head and make you feel like you might be a bit cocky because you're not worried.

You aren't crazy, and you aren't cocky. It's called being CONFIDENT in Christ. The devil will have you feeling all types of ways because you are standing on God's word. Don't let him shake you, stand firm.

Never let the limited views of others stop you from what you want to achieve.

A lot of people put their dreams on hold or throw them out of the window because they listen to naysayers or people that tell them to "be realistic."

Remember this...a carriage moving without horses was 'unrealistic.' People flying like birds was 'unrealistic.' Pyramids, skyscrapers, rollercoasters, they were all 'unrealistic' at some time in the past, but not today.

Hold your dreams, and don't let people who can't see the stars tell you they aren't there when you're looking through a telescope.

Be encouraged.

I know it is hard living when it seems that every obstacle around you wants you to do just the opposite, lie down and die. Don't fall into the trap. When you feel like giving up, don't. Know that whatever it is that is in your way right now has an expiration date. Trouble doesn't last always, and there is sunshine after the storm(s).

You give life to anything that you focus on. So while it seems like all you can see is destruction and no way up right now, focus on the way out and it will become more feasible to get out. Don't keep resuscitating the disparaging things around you, or energizing the negative aspects of your life. Revive the good. Hold onto the positive! Let those be your guiding light.

Think positive thoughts.

Thinking positively leads to feeling positive, which leads to living a positive life.

Positivity builds a healthy mentality, as well as healthy relationships. Nobody likes to be around, let alone friends with, Negative Nancy. They want people around that give off positive vibrations and that always have uplifting things to say.

Positive thinking always takes you up. How did Peter Pan fly...by thinking happy thoughts. He knew it would uplift his mind, body, and spirit.

Slow progress is still PROGRESS.

The world today is so fast-paced that we feel the need to mimic it.

We look at our biological clock and try to sync it with those around us. Bobby and Sue just got married...I'm not even dating...I must be a failure. Ron and Jill are on baby number two...you get the point?

Look around you! Not at everyone else, YOU! Where you are is where you are supposed to be at this present moment. Do your thing, and as long as it's doing something and you remain focused, your time will come. Pinky promise.

The most effective leaders are the ones that realize that they don't have all of the answers.

As moms, entrepreneurs, businesswomen, etc. we want to make sure we have solutions to problems and questions that are sure to arise.

The main thing to remember is that we will not always have every answer in the book of life. Humble yourself enough to ask questions when need be. If someone requests info from you, they will respect you more if you say, "I'm not sure, but I can certainly find out for you" rather than just giving flat-out wrong information because you don't want to look inferior since you didn't know AT THAT TIME.

Your reflections

Can you think of a time when you had a boss, teacher, or elder that thought they knew it all? How did it make you feel? Did you ever correct them when they were wrong, or did you just let them think that they were right? Was there ever a time that they were wrong and admitted it or apologized for it? Have you ever come up with a wrong answer and had to admit it or apologize for it? How did you feel afterwards?

Reflect below.

_____
_____
_____
_____
_____
_____
_____
_____
_____
_____
_____

Don't worry about the size of your circle decreasing, as long as the value is INCREASING.

Some people can't stand to see your success. Sometimes it's jealousy; sometimes it pushes them to look at what they are doing, or not doing, to the point it just pushes them right out of your life.

Don't look down on them! Don't feel bitter because their season is up in your life. Love them from a distance, appreciate the good times, and thank them for making room for valuable people and awesome life lessons.

I got you, but on one condition...

"I am here for whatever you need…as long as it is not that…or that…or…"

We hear this often, and it can act as a big discourager which makes you feel you don't need anyone else. It is a way for you to try doing it all by yourself. Well, I am here to tell you that if you can fulfill a dream by yourself, the dream is not big enough.

It could be quite possible that the people you are requesting assistance from just aren't meant to go with you on this journey. It could also be possible that the help you seek from them just isn't the capacity that they are supposed to assist you in. Don't count out everyone that gives you a no. No could simply mean 'not right now.'

Give applause where it's due.

Clap for those around you that experience success because when it is your time to shine you won't want your audience to fall silent.

A great trick of the devil is to give you a feeling of inadequacy.

Failed business ventures, relationships holding on by a thread, feelings of worthlessness; all of them and the likes can make it so easy for the devil to get into your head. He knows your weaknesses. He knows your faults. What he doesn't know, though, is just how strong your faith is and that you will rather listen to the promises of the Lord than the lies from *him*.

Never let minor setbacks make you feel like a failure. Never let temporary feelings put you in a bad enough place that you completely give up on your destiny. The devil cannot win if you fight.

If you are unhappy with little, you won't be blessed with much.

Over and over again we hear, 'count your blessings.' Over and over again we also hear people complain on a daily basis. We might even do it, too. Car troubles make us upset, but do you have the funds to get it fixed? Health problems come up, but do you have health insurance to go visit the doctor? Sometimes we have to take a step back and really look at the small blessings that we do have, really appreciate them, and show gratitude for them. Why would God bless you with a new car if you can't even be thankful for the means of transportation you have? At least you aren't walking. And if you are walking, thank God for the working limbs that get you to and from.

The more ungrateful we are, the more closed our hands are in God's eyes. How can He bless you with something new if your hands aren't open to receive it?

Forgive.

Who are we to not show mercy to ones that have wronged us, when we wrong God every day, and every day we are allowed grace and favor in our lives? Forgiveness is our way of saying, 'no matter what you have done to me I am better than the card you tried to deal me, and I am coming out victorious and what you do afterward is all on you.'

We should never be too bitter to be better. Being better is forgiving wrongs. Forgive for your sanity; forgive for your health; but most importantly, forgive because God forgives you.

Your reflections

Think of a time in your life where you had to accept and apology you never got. Now think of a time that you were supposed to give an apology that you never gave. How did each make you feel? Did you forgive anyway? Did you forgive yourself?

Reflect below.

_____
_____
_____
_____
_____
_____
_____
_____
_____
_____
_____
_____
_____
_____

You can't insult and inspire at the same time.

Have you ever received a compliment but it was suddenly ruined by a 'but?' Example, "I love your hair, girl, but I'm not sure about that color." Which part sticks out in your mind more: the fact that your hair is the bomb or the fact that the color is not becoming of you? The latter part, right?

You can't encourage someone and pass harsh judgment on them and expect them to be better or do better. Think about your words and be sure they are always uplifting. You never know what someone may be going through. Instead of telling her that her alcohol problem will be her demise, encourage her in some way to stop drinking so much or to get help. Let her know you will be there every step of the way, or help her see that she can get through the issue. Apply it to all issues someone might face…from a simple bad haircut to a major life concern, be encouraging.

Tomorrow is a new day.

The sun will set, but it will rise again; birthing a new day of opportunities. Yesterday is gone, and it does not matter now that we were not able to achieve our goals, the mere fact that we can see a tomorrow is proof that we weren't made to give up on them just yet. So, look to the days ahead and finish the race. A new day means a new opportunity for you to make a difference.

Let your actions speak for you more than your mouth does.

The only way to be a person of your word is through action. We can make promises all day, but if we never see them through people will start to doubt everything that comes out of our mouths. Saying you will get it done and getting it done are two majorly different things. Be a doer, not just a 'sayer.' Make good on your words.

Move in silence.

Think of a ninja; he gets more accomplished moving stealthily and unheard than someone who runs and yells towards his enemies, letting them know he is coming.

By announcing your every move, your haters will know what you're up to, and before you know it, that idea you think is unique to you, the next person gets it done before you and claims it as their own. It is acceptable to announce to get opinions of those closest to you that you trust the most, but when you broadcast your next chapter to the world via social media or the likes, either haters will down you, someone can pray against your success, or people will downright get tired of hearing your news.

For every one person that hopes you do, there are three that hope you don't.

Not everyone we think is for us is in fact for us. We have people in our circle clapping in our faces while secretly hoping for a fall flat on our face. It is ok to fall, and yes they will briefly have something to talk about. However, you better get back up and stun them all with an amazing comeback. Haters have no place in your higher callings.

Allow your present self to step aside and let your future self do what she needs to do.

It can be a very difficult process to embrace change, but it is even more difficult when the thing that is changing is you. We sometimes try so hard to fight the inevitable change we undergo within ourselves when we actually begin to grow as a person. We try to hold on to the old person that we grew to love and are so comfortable with, and sometimes that complacency is what keeps us stuck.

Sometimes you have to step outside of your old self and step into the new you in order to access the next level of purpose in your life. It is OK to be afraid, but embrace the scary and give her a chance. She is the only way you can accomplish those future goals.

Believing powerful lies leads to substantial consequences.

The devil tells many lies, and the most powerful ones that we tend to listen to are:
1) You are not loved.
2) You are not worthy or deserving.
3) You should just settle for less.

No! No! No! Cover your ears, put in a headset, hum a loud tune to drown him out, but whatever you do, don't listen to the hype.

God so loved the world…I am fearfully and wonderfully made…I know the plans I have for you…a future and a hope…We have our affirmations in God. We don't have to believe any tricks of the devil because God tells us differently. Believe that!

Who are you to tell yourself that you won't amount to anything?

How dare you pretend you know the outcome of you? How dare you sit around and tell yourself what you cannot do?

You lie to yourself on a daily basis…

-I can't do this

-This is too difficult (the load is too much for me to bear)

-I'll never change

You should tell yourself to shut up and affirm what it is you can do, what you will do, what you are capable of doing. Then, let's just wait and see who is right.

If it was easy, everybody would do it.

Your purpose is for you alone. Someone is waiting especially for you and the gifts you have to offer the world. A long road ahead, and a difficult one as well, but we can't let that stop us. Not everyone has answered the call to reach their destiny. Not everyone has the heart to pursue their dreams. Not everyone has the tenacity or bravery you possess because not everyone can do what you are meant to do.

If they don't lift you, drop them.

We can have everyone and their mothers in our corner, but what are they all there for? If they can't offer you encouraging words, if they can't support you on your new venture, or if they are only lurking to see if you fail, why are you keeping them around? Yes we are stuck with family, but there is nothing wrong with keeping your distance from the negative ones…it's all about knowing when to choose your battles, well in this case, interactions.

BECAUSE I AM WOMAN: *Reflections of a Woman*

Your reflections

Are there people in your circle that you KNOW shouldn't be there but you just can't seem to let them go? What is holding you back? Is it the longevity of the relationship? Is it because they are family? Is it because you feel like you owe them something because they have been down his long? Do you think you could ever drop the "dead weight?"

Reflect below.

_____
_____
_____
_____
_____
_____
_____
_____
_____
_____
_____
_____

JESSICA WOODRUFF

You do it then!

We hear too often, or even say it ourselves, 'something should be done about [insert issues here].' We all want to bring up the concern, but never want to give a solution to the problem. Better yet, we never want to BE the solution to the problem. Sometimes it takes more than just a call to Congress…sometimes you have to campaign and BE Congress. True we can't save the world, but instead of complaining about domestic or foreign issues, why not do anything, big or small, that we can to help alleviate the problem. You have an issue with it and nobody is acting on it like you want, YOU DO IT THEN!!!

Life is much grander when you focus on your destination rather than the reasons you are afraid to get there.

    Fear has kept you stuck long enough. Fear of failure, fear of success, fear of change. Push those reservations to the back of your mind, and go for your purpose. Being afraid of every little difference you will encounter is nonsense because every new day is a change from the last. The final destination will always be more worth the obstacles you encounter, so do it and enjoy the scenery when you arrive.

Dream big, then take even bigger action.

It will do no good to aspire to greatness and not back up those aspirations with massive action. Big dreams require hard work and determination for their achievement. Don't be intimidated by the workload and just give up. The reward for what you accomplish will be great when you go big and stick it out.

Sometimes people outgrow you, and you have to be ok with that.

    You can't say a person no longer loves or cares for you just because you no longer fit into the same role in their life. You hurt a while, but you pick up the pieces and move on. Trying to fit in somewhere you no longer belong can be too discomforting. Growing up, I had a favorite pair of Guess jeans...they were a size 8...one summer, I shot up (and out) and tried to get back in them. No deal. They were no longer comfortable to me. I had outgrown them. I had to get rid of them, but I was all right with that choice.

    Why? Because I knew that once they were no longer a good fit for me, and it was time to go for something newer and better for me. It's ok to get rid of the old that you have outgrown in order to usher in the new.

Sometimes the only way to GO through, is to GROW through.

Some lessons God places in our lives don't lead to a "final destination." Some lessons we may feel like we keep learning over and over again and we wonder what the purpose may be. Take a step back and really look at the situation. You could be "stuck" in that situation with nowhere to go because He has planted you there to prosper in that one place.

Grow through the situation! Be grounded like a great oak and flourish until it is time for the next lesson. Remember, tumbleweeds go places, too, and most times, it is just because they are wandering aimlessly.

JESSICA WOODRUFF

Woman Up! Don't expect credit for what you are supposed to do anyway.

Often times we see women who seek attention for things they should do anyway. "Look at me. I helped my child with his homework." "Check me out; I'm going to work." The simple things; things women should do anyway on a daily basis. Work hard and achieve your goals. If no one watches you in the process or acknowledges your hustle, so what? They will all see when you make it, and achieving greatness should be enough acknowledgment.

Instead of hating, use the moment to pray we all make it.

There's a place of victory reserved for us all, so why waste energy being hateful of others when we can use that strength to achieve our goals? Everyone is fighting a battle, either within oneself or forces from the outside. So instead of putting down the next person or abhorring her success, let us hope we can all overcome the isolating forces, and all be great!

Just keep going.

A few years back, I joined a network marketing business. I jumped in super excited, but that excitement died quickly. Why? There was no support from family or friends fast enough for me. So I quit. Months later I started receiving social media messages and calls about the product the venture offered. I could not help them because I had given up.

Another business venture, same results, same actions. This time, after efforts of selling products to family and friends and without any one of them wanting the product, I quit. Months later, what did I see? Friends posting pictures of themselves with the same product which they had bought FROM SOMEONE ELSE.

Then came my big dream. And of course, the devil stays in your ear when you are pursuing goals that better you and bring you closer to God. Right? So here he is, in my head like, "If they didn't support your small businesses, what makes you think they will support your big dream?"

He was almost right. Posts on social media, little to no response. Holding interest meetings, little response. Volunteer outings for my organization, the same few people would come every month, but no one else. Frustration was setting in, and setting in hard.

But I couldn't give up on this one. I could not quit. The other businesses were, for the most part, for personal gain. True, it would help the family save money, or friends healthwise, but in the long run, it was financial gain in my pocket. This was far greater than I, bigger than myself.

So I decided to keep going. Even if I had one attendee at an empowerment retreat. Even if I had 5 attendees at a women's conference. I was highly determined to JUST KEEP GOING, and you should never give up either.

Don't give in to peer pressure; create it (positively of course).

Remember as a teenager, or even a young kid, friends tried to get you to do the craziest things. Depending on the crowd you hung around, crazy could have meant dangerous or crazy could have meant silly. Remember the feeling that if you did not do it, they would be disappointed in you or you felt like they would not call you a friend anymore.

We should get back to those days, but in a positive way. Challenge your girlfriends, even guy friends, to do something daring. Not saying bet them to jump off the roof of the house, but triple dog dare them (Ooooh!!! Steps back, aghast) to do something bold, like start a business, set out to accomplish that dream they told you about eons ago, or write a book. Make them feel like if they do not at least try it, you won't stop being their friend or make fun of them, but let them feel the pressure by holding them accountable with completing the goal. Let's call it The Positive Peer Pressure Challenge. Are you ready for it?

When they say you can't make it, start making it.

Nothing feels better than to prove a hating, bitter, no-goal-having, loathe when others succeed, miserable person wrong. Especially when they try to tell you that you cannot do anything. When they try to discourage you, it's usually because they did not/ do not have the courage to go after that big dream they wanted/want. So, their vision stays in their thought bubble, festering, fading away while they still hope to erase yours before it even gets started in your mind.

DO NOT LET THEM WIN! Make it happen, and make it happen in a big way. Never wish negativity on them though. Just pray that they get their act together and find the courage and will to succeed, all while fulfilling your God-given purpose…making yourself, and God, look good!

Your blessing is on the other side of your release. Let go...

Oftentimes we hold on to something so hard in fear that if we let it go we will never receive anything that may be better than that. We would rather stay in a hurtful place because we know it and are complacent there than to move on to better things that are more comfortable and fitting for our purpose.

Then sometimes we hold on to something because we feel like if we let it go, our identity may go with it. That job because of the title it brings, that relationship because of...well...the title it brings, too, and so on. Let go, let loose, and open your hands to receive the next blessing. Not knocking anyone's livelihood, but the title of CEO could look way better on you. Not knocking anyone's situation, but the title of wife sounds much better than baby mama forever, right?

It's not how high we are that scares us; the thought that we may fall gives us pause.

Think about the fear you have…dogs, the dark, heights? Now, rationally think of why you are afraid of it. If the fear has to do with dogs, it's not the mere sight of them that terrifies you, is it? No…it's the potential of them biting you, mauling you, scratching you even. The same for the dark…it's not that it hurts you, per se, but the fear of the unknown, while you are in a dark place, is what gets to you. Is there someone or something lurking? Will I be attacked unknowingly before I can put up a defense? The same can be said for heights. It is not really being up high that makes your knees wobble and shake and causes you to feel sick to your stomach, but the fact that you may lose your footing way up there and fall to your demise.

I say all of that, to say this: people do not fear success. They fear the outcome of success, they fear the journey of success, and they fear the changes that come with success. The thought of being pushed out of their comfort zones; the what-ifs of if they don't reach the level of success that others hold them up to; the surroundings that they are used to at this present moment that will feel so uncomfortable and foreign once they reach the top of their game. Those are what they fear.

Don't let the fear of the unknown stop you from chasing what you KNOW to be your divine purpose. Use fear to help you move FORWARD, ELEVATE, ARISE, and REJOICE.

Because yes, we don't know what is at the end of the journey to success, but we do know that growth and knowledge are good pit stops.

One day you'll wake up, and it will all make sense.

Remember the times your parents would tell you to do something (or not do something), and you just couldn't understand why they were saying it? It was so frustrating, but as you grew older and (what you thought) wiser, it began to make sense why your mom always told you not to (insert mother's warning here).

Just like the wisdom of our parents started to make sense seemingly all of a sudden, so will the workings and doings of GOD in your life begin to make sense as well. He kept you out of that city for a reason. He kept you from that job for a reason. He kept you out of that relationship for a reason. When the knowledge of why hits you, all you may be able to do is shout "Thank You!" You may not know what He is up to right now, but one day it will all make sense.

BECAUSE I AM WOMAN: *Reflections of a Woman*

Your reflections

Has any reflection stood out for you thus far? What were your initial feelings when you read it? Was it a word or a read, sis? Do you think you can follow the advice?

Reflect below.

_____
_____
_____
_____
_____
_____
_____
_____
_____
_____
_____
_____
_____
_____
_____
_____
_____

Trust me when I say, their approval does not matter.

So many times I felt myself doubting what I should be doing at a particular time in my life, worrying about what the next person would say. What have you worried about in your life?

I need to take this second job, but it's just fast food…will my friends make fun of me?

I have to get around separately from my spouse, but we can't afford a new car, and the only other way to get around is public transportation. Will people think I am poor because I am on the bus?

My children can't stay at home by themselves, and I can't afford daycare right now. If I leave them with their grandparents will my family see me as an irresponsible parent?

You might ask yourself these questions. Do you know what your answer should be? SO WHAT? As long as you are bettering yourself for your future and your children, the opinion of others should be the last thing on your mind. Focus on what God will say when you complete the task He has assigned to you. Will He say, "Well done?" That is all that matters in the end.

People won't know who you are unless you tell them (fake it 'til you make it).

I have been in a few businesses, and yes it is wrong to deceive others, but I have seen people dress up in suits and speak eloquently like they were high-ranking business owners but they had only been in the business for a few months. Guess who developed a large following after speaking in front of the crowd like they owned it?

Life is based a lot on perception. If you want to be a CEO, boss, or leader, dress and act to par. You may not be the owner of a Fortune 500 Company (YET), but who has to know that? Present yourself as such, and others will believe it. You will believe it, and that makes it achievable.

It's important to know that you will face trials and tribulations. It is even more important to know that God will see you through them.

    Everyday obstacles can sometimes leave us feeling like we are all alone in our pursuit of greatness. We deal with stresses all the time, but somehow and some way we get through them.
    Look to the Heavens from whence cometh your help. God will see you through the toughest times. Even when it seems as if there is no light at the end of the tunnel or that the tunnel will be never ending, God has a way to show us that He will be beside us every step of the way. And when we can no longer walk, He will carry us through. We just have to keep the faith through it all.

No day is guaranteed, but life is. How are you living yours?

People say, "Live every day like it's your last." I say, instead, live life like you're trying to make a difference. If you wake up every day using your God-given talents and abilities to live out your purpose, you will move on to the next realm having accomplished something. If you wake up every day with the intent of making a difference in the life of at least one other person, you will leave an impact on the world you leave behind.

It's not about looking forward to your last day on earth; it's about living in the moment of the time that you still have and using the precious moments to leave a legacy that is worth something behind.

Until you follow God's path for you, you will feel like you are walking in circles.

We all have a divine purpose in life, but how will we achieve it if we don't follow a divine path? Obstacles and trials will always come into our lives, but how will we know how to navigate around them as speed bumps instead of having them halt us in our tracks like stop signs if we don't follow our divine path? A heaven-sent vision deserves a heaven-sent guide, and that guide is the Lord. Follow Him!

From here on out, it gets better.

    Think of the rain showers we see often...what follows? Well, besides the humidity here in the south, it's sunshine and blue skies, right? Why should your life be any different?

    Why not know that after that breakup, someone better for you is coming...after being let go from your job, more doors will be open unto you...after losing so much already, blessings will be flooding your way, and you will receive double for your troubles?

    However, you have to believe this in order to receive this. And favor beyond your comprehension will manifest in your life.

    Will you believe it? Will you receive it?

Be exceptional, not "acceptional."

People always look to be accepted but don't try to stand out from the crowd. Learn to be exceptionally great, rather than "acceptionally" fit in. No, that may not be a word, but if a definition could be put to it, it would read something like, "The need to feel wanted, to belong, or to be accepted by all costs."

We should live our lives in an exceptional manner so that people will follow our names with "except you." From an early age, teach your children to be exceptional. "Everyone was talking when the teacher was talking, EXCEPT YOU." "Everyone skipped school to do lewd behavior, EXCEPT YOU." "Everyone went out partying last night instead of studying for the finals, EXCEPT YOU." Then as adults, we will learn to live exceptionally, possess exceptional character traits, have exceptional work ethics, and make exceptional impacts on others.

When was the last time you told someone that you were proud of them?

Women go through life showing support for everyone around them. We make sure all is taken care of with our homes; family is fed, children are clean, and spouses are happy. When someone does amazing things, we are usually the first to congratulate them. Our children make the honor roll; we are right there to cheer them on as they walk across the stage to receive their little certificate. If our spouse gets that promotion they are up for; we are there making that celebratory dinner to honor their accomplishment. We give and give and do not really want anything in return other than the knowledge that our loved ones are happy, secure, and well taken care of.

However, when was the last time you genuinely looked at another woman and told her that you were proud of her? Think about it. For holding down this home while your husband drives his truck across country all week; for getting up and getting things done even when every bone or muscle in your body tells you to "lie down for 30 more minutes;" or for not giving up even with all odds against you, the societal doubts being thrown at you, the stereotypical obstacles placed in front of you, and the inner qualms that you even place upon yourself.

Let someone know you are so proud of the woman that they are and the woman that they are working to be. You never know if that could be the push that they needed to keep going. You also never know if whatever God has in store for them to accomplish will benefit you or maybe your future generation.

Someone is waiting for you.

Someone is searching for the person that you will become. Whether it is someone searching for a wife to be equally yoked with, a forever friend to share secrets with, or a mentor to learn from, there is someone out there that needs you. There is someone out there that needs the person that God knows you will become.

The tests will make you a stronger leader, and the setbacks will build character and show people around you that are watching that they, too, can get through anything, regardless of the circumstances. Someone out there needs you to keep pushing because the you that is coming out of the fire, the you that is emerging from the ashes, the you that is being polished will make a world of difference for someone that needs you.

Your reflections

We never truly know how our life's purpose could impact the people we are intended to benefit. Regardless of our understanding, someone is depending on us to complete our mission. What is one thing you look to accomplish and what impact do you hope it will have on others? What impact do you hope it will have on you?

Reflect below.

_____
_____
_____
_____
_____
_____
_____
_____
_____
_____
_____
_____
_____

Learn to pray for need, not want.

Often times we ask God for the things we THINK we need, but are actually a longing desire or deep want that we have. And we can't be too hard on ourselves when we do it because we are going off the Word, or at least what we interpret it, understand it to mean, and have been told it means. "God shall supply all of my needs according to His riches and glory in Christ Jesus" ....

We miss a lot when we don't pray for true understanding of this verse. 1) The Word does not say that God will give us what we really, really want if we just believe, but instead, He gives us what we need to not only fulfill whatever purpose He has for us in life, but also to achieve that purpose in order to glorify His kingdom. 2) Our needs are very different from our wants. It is up to us to not only decipher the two, but also discern when and how to ask for them.

For instance, we come into trials and tribulations often in our lives. These could be financial situations, marital problems, sickness, etc. And when we pray, what do we pray for? "Lord, please take this back pain away." Or "Lord, bless my finances and the finances of my household and of those that can hear the sound of my voice right now, Lord God." But what of the times when we find ourselves right back in the same predicaments? We should not have prayed for a financial blessing. Sounds crazy right? But it's not. Instead, we should have prayed for the skills to be a good steward of the finances that He has already given us so that we would not end up back in the same boat, or we should have prayed for the knowledge and wisdom to see and know how we are frivolously spending (if it applies) and ask for the skill- and mind-set of someone who knows how to properly handle their funds, spend on what is really needed, and invest in a way that our money can work for His kingdom and ourselves. See the difference?

Focus on the GOOD and watch GOD show up!

I like to simply sum this up by saying praise Him anyhow. Despite what it looks like now, take a step back and see if you can find the blessing in the lesson. Good can come out of all situations. Life is not always sunshine and rainbows, but guess what…that rain that's pouring down is nourishing something and helping it grow. You may not be able to see the beautiful blue skies through the downpour right now, but try to see the beauty of the rain washing away the unnecessary. How we see it is, we may not always have the best of days, but regardless of it all, thank Him anyway.

It's easier to just cut off the dead weight than to let it hold you back from your destination.

    Be careful of the friends…correction, associates, that will hold onto your coat tail for as long as you let them simply because they know you are going somewhere. They aren't doing anything to benefit you. They are just waiting for you to make a move with the hope that you will drag them along for the ride. They watch as you put in all of the hard work, let you do all of the sweating and back-bending, and then, are quick to say, "We made it," when you get to your destiny.

    Imagine you are walking through a dense forest, not really aware of what is coming in front of you next, but you just know you need to get to where you are going, and you need to get there speedily. However, holding onto your shirt are the people who want to use you to get to 'glory' without putting in any effort of their own or without helping the team get out of darkness. They slow you down; they let you run into spider webs all by yourself and say to you "Girl, we almost got caught up in some mess, huh? Glad you saw that coming because I cannot get grossness in my hair." They watch as tree branches smack you in the face. They nitpick when you stumble over a rock or an unforeseen hole.

    When you realize it is best to cut them off, the ones that don't just fall off on their own anyway because the forest is a bit too dirty for them, you can not only make room on your own to place a survivor's backpack on your back filled with encouraging counterparts, but also get knowledge of the area of expertise you are dealing in, as well as some rope to throw to someone who will put in some effort to help you climb out of that quicksand you landed in instead of watching you sink. When you drop them, my God, the places you will go!

Sometimes convenience can cost you.

Why is it that we sometimes only take heed to God's answers to questions or prayers when it is CONVENIENT for us? We get the message plain as day and we are like, "Ooh, nope, that wasn't for me; let me keep praying on it…" The only reason we don't take heed being the fact that it isn't the answer that our flesh wants, so we go with what our flesh tells us to, or we do nothing at all. But isn't doing nothing just as bad as going against the will of God, if what He says calls us to take action regardless of how hard it may be, how much support from family we lack, or how much confidence in ourselves we don't have? Wouldn't you rather follow His will and stay true to His word that everything works for the greater good? Would it not be better to make it through the trials knowing your outcome would be victory regardless of the process?

Suffer through what you might feel as an "inconvenience" now instead of living a life of disobedience.

Again I say, keep going!

After so many failed endeavors, fruitless attempts, and road blocked dreams, when do you just throw in the towel and give up? NEVER! Keep pushing, keep fighting, change routes, and keep going. The end. Period.

You are one step closer to success when you make the decision to try.

    The first step is admitting it. Admitting you have somewhere to go and admitting to yourself that you will get up and try to reach that destination. All it takes is an effort from you to say, "Yes. I will get up off of my butt and at least try."

    If all else fails, at least you can say you gave it your all and tried instead of sitting back watching and waiting. Your attempt is more than some people will ever do. Be proud of your effort.

To stop taking chances is a sure fire way to run out of them.

This plays off of the quote, "You miss every shot that you don't take." We are given chance after chance to make something right or to succeed in our endeavors. Chance after chance we miss our mark and feel like we blew it. So, we give up. It's not that we have run out of chances because we get as many as we take. We run out of faith to keep going.

The only thing holding you back is the chance you aren't taking.

Guard your heart. Guard your dreams.

Hearts and dreams should be guarded with the same caution. Both are a sacred piece of you, and if you find someone who not only protects your heart with their all, but also guards your dream as if it is their own, keep them.

You wouldn't pitch an idea to someone who didn't have the capital to invest in it, would you? So why will you give your heart to someone who doesn't intend to invest in you? Why will you share your dreams with someone who has no interest in your life goals?

People that are genuine are a rare find. If they don't love you for what is in your heart and what is in your soul and what you dream to accomplish, don't waste your time.

BECAUSE I AM WOMAN: *Reflections of a Woman*

Your reflections

Dreams are sweetest when we can pursue and accomplish them, and even sweeter when we have someone to share them with. Who is that one person that you always think of first when you get good news or are about to embark on a new journey? Do they support your dreams? Do they bring you back to Earth when the ream gets a bit too lavish?

Reflect below.

_____
_____
_____
_____
_____
_____
_____
_____
_____
_____
_____
_____

Take a look around you and know that your current situation is not your final destination.

God places us in situations for different reasons. Sometimes it is to grow us, sometimes it is to mold us, and sometimes it is to say, "Not yet." When you are in a season that is not ideal for your destiny, don't be discouraged. Keep in mind that it is only temporary and learn the lessons that are being taught to you at that moment. Take it in strides, and know that the day will come when you will be living out your purpose and achieving those big dreams.

Release it to the right One.

    I think it's ok to cry it out, scream it out, and let it all out somehow. I don't believe it shows that you have lost faith.
    No, I think it shows quite the opposite. I think it shows that you put your faith in yourself to do things that should have been handed over a long time ago and now with you releasing that 'built up-ness' it has nowhere else to go but to the ONE that was supposed to be dealing with it in the beginning. Let go and give it to the only ONE that can make it alright. Release!

Words of encouragement are free.

With so much going on in everyone's lives and so much going on in the world, people are resorting to second jobs, crowdfunding websites, and even begging on the streets. And while others are asking for help, some of us are on the brink of having to ask ourselves…so how in the world could we possibly help someone else when we can barely afford to help ourselves? I always say, kind words are better than nothing at all.

We may see a friend set up a crowdfunding website asking for car repair help or charity for their children's upcoming fall football league, and although we may love the children and say we will do anything for our dear friend, money around our household may be a tad bit tight at that moment. One thing that's better than completely running from them, if we genuinely do not have any financial help to offer them, is spiritual help. An encouraging word and moral support definitely go a longer way than us showing we are not truly a friend when we run away.

It is ok to falter, as long as you don't lose faith.

Sometimes I feel bad about worrying or doubting for the small amount of time I do. Then I tell myself as long as I can shake it off and keep the faith, I am good. Peter walked every day with Jesus, and even *he* faltered for a little while as he began to sink into the sea. Sometimes you just need that cold water on your feet to snap you back onto your path of faith. God is good; even when you can't immediately see the plan, it is there. Shake off the temporary doubt and keep to it. Faith dissipates fear.

Sometimes you have to disconnect in order to reconnect.

We live in a society of distractions, distractions, distractions!!! Every other month there is a new form of social media, and we rush to download it onto our phones, knowing the other four or five social media outlets that we already have usually take up more than half of our day. From scrolling to posting to liking and commenting, we spend a lot of time being nosey and little time working on our dreams or even working on ourselves. If we aren't being social on social media, some of us are being social on our phones. Texting with friends, chatting with associates, but not doing enough of the things like setting up business appointments or scheduling time for networking events.

We have to get back to our center. Disconnect from the distractions of the outside world and reconnect to the things that drive us to be better. Get back in touch with our own passions instead of living vicariously through celebrities that post trips, share their homes, or make videos of them living their dreams. We have to rediscover the things that get us closer to our God-given purpose on this earth, and if that means unplugging from the outside diversions, then let's do it!

Learn from your mistakes; don't be defined by them.

We all have made mistakes in life. We have all had a hard-taught lesson or two, but look at you. Look at me; we're still pushing, we have not let that mistake tell us who we will be.

Think of the legend of the Phoenix. We know her not because she burns, but because of her ability to rise from the ashes. She emerges from what life throws her way as beautiful as ever. Her new gorgeous feathers represent her new found confidence and are her way to push forward. So you take those scars of your past mistakes and use them as a way to push yourself forward and out of the past now that you have learned to rise from the ashes.

We have to learn to let go.

Ladies, ladies, ladies…baggage is a sure way to be held back or slowed down. We have to learn to let it go, and I mean let it ALL go.

The grudge you are holding for your ex-husband, release it. The bitterness you feel for your baby's father because he has a new woman around your children, toss it (don't be a bitter baby mama). The self-doubt that presses against you every time you are about to put yourself out there, ignore it. The feelings of despair that creep in when you feel like you aren't where you need to be, forget them and remember this season is temporary.

We hold on to so much negative energy and emotions that it is hard for us to open up to blessings and positivity that God is trying to place in our lives. Learn to let go and let in what He has in store for you.

Succeed anyhow.

Ladies, we are all in battle with one common enemy, and that is systemic sexism. You know, glass ceilings, lower wages, etc.

Even with all that we have against us, we must never give up. We have to look adversity in the face and succeed anyhow. We have to stare down our fears and succeed anyhow. We have to climb over those barriers and succeed anyhow.

And congratulate your sister. Be happy for your friend. Even if there's something that you are doing and they choose to go with the next, we're all winning if one of us is winning. We have to believe that wholeheartedly because if we don't, we'll get up the ladder of success and step on the fingers of those coming up behind us instead of grabbing their hand and pulling them up, too. Success is accomplished through sisterhood, so fight together and SUCCEED ANYHOW!

Your reflections

If there was one thing you could do knowing you would not fail doing it, what would it be? Have you tried to do it? If not, what has held you back from doing so? If you have tried it, what obstacles have stood in the way of your success? Did you give up when you lost your footing, or are you just adjusting for a great comeback?

Reflect below.

_____
_____
_____
_____
_____
_____
_____
_____
_____
_____
_____
_____
_____

JESSICA WOODRUFF

www.ingramcontent.com/pod-product-compliance
Lightning Source LLC
Chambersburg PA
CBHW061743040426
42453CB00024B/590